A Fork

in the

Road

Wife, Caregiver, Widow

Ruby Daggett

ISBN 978-1-0980-7843-0 (paperback)
ISBN 978-1-0980-7844-7 (digital)

Christian Faith Publishing, Inc.
832 Park Avenue
Meadville, PA 16335
www.christianfaithpublishing.com

Printed in the United States of America

This book is about true facts of life as a wife, caregiver, and widow looking at the life of being with my husband Donnie as a strong backbone of his family. How life slowly drained him, a strong man to a man depending all on his wife, Ruby. The look of how he fought to keep his head above water and how his strength was always a struggle He learned how to stand on his prayers, and even though he wasn't physically able to do work outside the home, he lifted his family up in prayer. He was determined not to burden down and hurt his family to the extent of burdening them. This shows that the beginning of his road of the stroke was an up and down road going in and out of rehabs. How a wife coped while being a caregiver and still working a full-time job. How the going back and forth to rehabs with no outside help from family or professionals. How the upheaval of how the insurance company tried to cut him off his disability. The final event of how a long-term wife of thirty-nine years had to put her husband to rest having to take a separate lonely road without the physical help of family. Noticing how widows are treated by family and friends. Have a rude awakening that things are not the same. That family members ignore you before death, and surely the same thing happens after death. How the strength of God sustained both Donnie and Ruby to get through a day.

How Ruby didn't know the strength she had until Donnie became weak by making household decisions. How Ruby stayed focused while her husband was deteriorating before her eyes. While keeping the faith and still keeping it moving. This is not an odd or abnormal lifestyle; widows across the country are dealing with being caregivers for their spouse. They pull up their big girl draws and push on; they have to focus on "if not me, then who will help?" The answer is no one usually. This is part of my healing that I needed to do to free my thoughts and mind and use this to help the new widows that are coming behind me to let them know you are not going crazy if you experience any of these experiences.

How Do You Really Feel?

I feel like me and other widows/widowers have been kicked to the side and ignored and not recognized so mainly I am writing this book to speak for the ones that can't or won't speak for themselves. Do I want pity? No, I don't. What I do want people to know which I didn't know is that the majority of this road have women in it, and once you are a member in this group, these women are so supportive and understanding. We are still here, we are still standing, it might have been an easier and less rockier road if the ones that was placed in our lives the same time our husband was placed in our life would simply care enough to pick up a phone or drop a text to see how you are doing would have helped. Now I have to release so I can heal because this is a new season and I have to keep it moving. This is four years now if you haven't heard from them before, then stop looking. Moving on. That's how I really feel.

Disclaimer

This synopsis of times thoughts are times with other widows, times observing others, or my thoughts of personal times with my husband. It's a mixture up and mingling together of my life with others. The situations are true, but each person that are in the story have been changed to protect them. Don't focus on the individual, focus on the situation to help you walk through your journey to help you wobble through this maze of life. The stories could be me personally or Jackie or Sheila, but they are fact based. This is basically a way of helping you walk this journey now or this journey later.

Never thought I would be in this circumstance of being a caregiver. My children were grown and just me and my granddaughter Lelani and husband mainly. Being at home, never knew that his supervisor would call me, telling me, "We are walking him next door to the ER, his BP is very high." They did this twice. The last time he left work, he drove himself home. I didn't know he had a stroke at that time.

I am a looker, meaning I like to go to malls, and when I am at the restaurant, I look and stare not so the person can see I am observing. I have noticed that there are a lot of women that are in the position of care giving for their spouse. They make appointments for their husbands, they go on the doctor's appointments with their husband. Even before the full-blown caregiving stage, they are taking their husband to the doctors, making their doctor visits, going with them, like they would go with their elderly parents or their young children. When did this change of life happen? You know you really don't know or noticed a life change until it happens to you. There are a lot of women that are taking care of their husband or burying their husband.

I was a kept woman, meaning I didn't have to pay any bills in all the thirty-plus years of marriage my husband paid the bills. I didn't have any problem with that. He often told me get a bank account, but I was always saying later, later. Putting off things like that was not a wise thing to do. After he got a stroke, I didn't know my bills were late until I start getting calls from the bill collectors. Donnie paid all our bills online, so I had to figure out his password and accounts.

The first part of his disability was short-term funds, I borrowed one time from one of my kids until his short-term disability kicked in. I went through unnatural born hell with the rep at the insurance company. I had to verify each month that Donnie was still sick and disabled. The doctor's office was slow about getting the medical notes, and if the doctor's office is not open but three times a week, that was a problem. I would get threatening letters from the insurance company that if the notes didn't reach them in a timely manner that he would be cut off. So between the time of working, taking him to his doctor's visits, making appointments, and calling the doctor's office to make sure they get the notes to the insurance company was a total overload. Looking back at the first year of this change of life, I can see the hand of God holding me up and keeping me from having a nervous breakdown. This is a time in life when I needed to slow it down, but it was picking up for me. I am now living two lives, mine and my husband's.

I hate strokes; it changes the character of an individual for the good or bad. My husband had an up-down character as it is. Didn't know which way he was coming from day to day before the stroke. When my kids were in school, he went through a long time of being depressed. Other than going to work, he would stay in the bed depressed. I remember one time I was going to a church and it was so bad, I asked the pastor of that church if he could come and pray for my husband. His answer was "I will pass this request to my other associates, but I am busy with my family on Mondays."

I had never asked for anything from this ministry. I am not that type of person. I am not needy. Needless to say, that was the first and last time I asked. But God was looking over me in that situation come to find out the pastor was cheating on his wife at that time and that would have transferred that spirit to my family so that was God covering, I see now. Lesson learned, when things don't go the way you think they should, don't get mad that could be the way God is looking out for you, so nothing worse will happen to you down the road. Donnie's character is now humbling he is very appreciative, whereas before he was negative. He told me that the last year he worked, he would tell his coworkers, "I am getting out of this job." He had grown to hate, now he was talking about retiring or just leaving his job. But the way he said he didn't emphasize. Watch the words you say; the devil will turn them to the negative and the outcome is bad.

Donnie had many illness. I remember when my last child was going through his kindergarten graduation and my husband was fighting for his life in the hospital. On the way to the hospital, I heard the EMS talking on their phone, "We are bringing in a DOA."

His breathing was so shallow, bleeding inside, they didn't know where the bleeding was, and that was the onset of his many times in and out of the hospital. From over and over of hitting him in his back to slapping him out of unconsciousness from blood sugar being so low, he made it through the many times. Jesus touched his body, that's why I can't be mad at God; he healed and delivered when I touched God with prayer he delivered. Jesus brought Lazarus back to life, and later he died. Some of us think that when God heals us and deliver us that means death will not take us out ever. Not so.

I didn't know at first that Donnie had a stroke because his mouth was never turned to the side. He had a slight dragging of his foot. The enemy was really trying to take him out in 2012; he had a carpal tunnel and foot surgery that took one year to heal and a stroke and lastly on dialysis. This man now walks with a walker and gets mad when we make him walk daily. Oh yeah, he had a stint put in his arteries for clog arteries.

Now I have wondered how I went to questioning how in the world did we get here? We were good parents, stayed out of trouble, he worked two or three jobs to keep food on table and roof over our head. That is why I will do for him until I can't do no more, when we couldn't do, he did and never complained when he was younger. I remember when we came from Florida, we didn't have proper winter clothes, but he got a big coat and would walk through several blocks to get a bus in the nighttime. In situations like this, you don't look at the bad times of life, you focus on the good, and that will help you to stretch out to help and that give you strength to keep on going forth.

Do I feel like giving up? Yes, sometimes. I have a great daughter that when I get tired, she is there to help her father now as his caregiver. What do they say about your daughters, you might fight or fuss, but at the end, they will come when you need them the most. My daughter and my grands keep me grounded.

Is my husband the only one in his family? You know if I was blind, I would say yes. I remember a time two years ago when Donnie was in the hospital and his kidneys were going down. The doctor came in and said, "Mrs. Daggett, this is the time to get his family together if he has brother, sister, to tell them."

His sister Patsy and oldest brother Joe kept up with him; distance didn't stop them from checking on their brother. He didn't pass at that time. He came off the ventilator.

I have talked to women that have been caregivers for husbands, and one of them told me when your husband is in the hospital, don't sign any paperwork, let him sign if it is nothing but an X because if he passes, all the bills will be turned over to you. She had to file bankruptcy because of this.

Things we don't think of when everything but the kitchen sink is thrown at us, we have to be responsible for someone else's life and then take care of yourself.

My husband use to take all his meds, including his insulin, and he would know the time. Now I have to give it to him and make sure that his numbers are not too high or low.

Now how do you tell a stroke person to believe and have faith? Depending on the state of mind, they can't comprehend sometime. So I have to believe and push him to believe. He got born again couple months before his stroke so he didn't have his spiritual muscles built up at that time. I thought he was having a nervous breakdown; I didn't know it was a stroke. He was diagnosed with a TIA, a small stroke.

I remember when I was going through the first week of this ordeal, I was so overwhelmed with what was going on. I wanted to read God's word, but with my mind racing, I was only able to read one word, a couple of phrases that helped me get through at the end of the day. That's why we are to hide God's word within our hearts.

From Wife to Caregiver and Widow

I was married to Donnie for thirty-nine years; we had four kids and nine grandchildren together. You can say Donnie was a workaholic, not a bad way but in a way to support his family with a wife staying home, raising our children. All I had to do was make sure kids were fed, taken to school, and took them to their afterschool activities. It was okay to him that I was a full-time mother. If we needed extra money for children's needs, he would just ask for extra hours or get a part-time job. I never had to pay the bills, so he was working outside the home and also balancing the bills. I looked at the private school bills, three proms in a row, money for bowling leagues, baseball gear for kids, and braces for teeth. I look at all those funds leaving out the house and bills upon bills and hearing no complaints, just going out the door to punch another clock.

I rec'd the call from Donnie's supervisor on 4/12; she had to walk him over to the emergency room because his blood pressure was triple digit. This happened two days in a row. He tried to go back to work, but he couldn't keep up; no one knew at that time he had a stroke. I thought it was a nervous breakdown because of all the crying and anxiety. He would holler out at night and put his hand on my shoulder like a little boy when he was afraid someone was coming for him. He couldn't remember how to pay bills; he didn't know the necessity of money. All of this was at the beginning of the sickness.

****

Hey, don't worry. Keep it moving; there is a better day coming. Someone will come at your right and left side.

****

A stroke is an illness that will get rid of everybody in your life, the good people and the not so good. A stroke will make your brothers, sisters, uncles, aunts, children run for the hills. I can laugh about it now, but at the time, I wondered how can you neglect your relative like that? It's either fear, hurt, or selfishness; you have to laugh away the hurt because laughter is medicine.

****

Stop and breathe and take time out for yourself. You can't run when you are out of energy. So focus and get regenerated. Refuel.

****

Donnie started his short-term leave of absence to try to get himself together; he had carpal tunnel surgery and a foot surgery done and a heart stint done while on the leave. The foot surgery took over a year to recover from. During that time, he still kept getting on the foot against the doctor's order. I was at work and he was still driving and limping on his foot. After we visited one of our kids in Chicago, I noticed he was wobbling in and out the lanes and was not really looking before changing lanes. I had to ask him to pull over and let me drive back home. That was the last time he drove. When we got back, he started having high anxiety and the psychiatrist prescribed him some medication for anxiety. It was a small dose, but he would break the pills in half; he didn't want to get addicted. He would wake me up in the middle of the night for the medication because I had put it out of his way. This was like an addiction so I called a rehab to check him in; he was only on it for a short time. I call for two days to see if there was a bed available, and when they had a place available, I was able to take him; he stayed in there for two weeks because they made a determination that he was not addicted to this medication, his system was just so sensitive. When he came home, he didn't want to stay home by himself, so I had to take him to one of my sons' house in the morning before I went to work. I did that for about a week until we decided to move out of our home to an apartment. Before the stroke, I could never talk him to move out of his home but now nothing mattered.

Donnie's legs had start swelling so my son had start taking him to his doctor's visits after he was not able to drive himself. After his foot surgery, he still tried to maintain his own care. The doctor told him to stay off his debrided foot, but he couldn't stay still; he still would get in his truck. I had also begin starting to paying the bills; it dawned on me that he wasn't going on the computer to pay bills and things had started getting behind. I had never paid a bill and didn't know the password to the bank account. I was able to find all of the information on a small piece of paper in his checkbook. He was able to tell me about some accounts before he had totally forgot about the management of the bills. He had everything systematically written down on a paper on what bills were paid to the date. I was able to go right behind and pick up his system of paying bills. I was doing all of this on my check because his disability check had not started yet. One of my sons helped me. I usually don't like to ask for help, but this was unavoidable.

When Donnie's disability started from his job, I had to make sure that all of the office notes were sent in monthly or they always threatened to stop his check, so between working, setting up doctor's appointments to make sure they sent the notes to the insurance company, coming home to take care of his foot. I look at all of this now and get tired of thinking about everything that was on my plate. I am exhausted. When I was in the process of doing this, it was like auto pilot. I was just doing and not thinking about it. I just thank God for all the prayers that was holding me up doing this time.

Think Before You Abandon

Does a person that have had a stroke know how you feel (depending on the extent of the stroke)? Yes.

Does a person that have had a stroke miss loved ones? Yes.

Does a person that have had a stroke remember the past? Yes.

Does a person that have had a stroke voice their own opinion? Yes.

In my case, Donnie was not bedridden and he was able to still feed himself and use cup or bottle to drink. Thank God for that. This is a little information that people need to know just because a stroke was involved in our love one's life doesn't mean they don't feel or see they just articulate it differently. Don't just assume get to know how the person is functioning now. At the beginning of my husband's stroke, I used to kid him. You have no cognitive skills because he would do things without thinking first. Bursting out anything in front of anybody. Later on, he didn't do the bursting out as much. I remember at church one morning in the midst of the pastor giving the sermon he rolled out the church in his wheelchair, saying, "Boring." I hurried up and followed him out, hoping that no one heard him.

I asked the social worker if there was a group home or facility I could take my husband to while I was at work. She tells me to check the websites that they couldn't endorse a particular place. No help at all. Organizations are so scared of being sued that they are handicap to you. There is no place other than a place for seventy-plus-year-olds, not for the younger stroke patients. I asked Donnie did he want to go, but he didn't want to be with all the elderly, no one was his age. Also I didn't know until a year after my husband's disability that I could have been on FMLA, which made it much better to get Donnie back and forth to doctor's visits.

I Can't Go On

Just when you think that all is not going well and you feel like all odds are against you. This is the time to reflect on the good times of before. When you and good times memories and pictures are everything. Memories, pictures, and good times get you through the bad times.

Tired

This maybe the middle of the day for you and you have to decide on what to pay, balancing the checkbook; you are doing this all by yourself with no help. When will this negative end in my life? Does God see me, do my loved ones see me going through, or do they care? God has not left you. He is so near when others are so far.

Unloved

I have to give that extra push, that extra love, because their other close loved ones have walked out of their life. They didn't make a formal announcement that they are no longer in the equation, but when there are no phone calls and no letters or cards, it is very evident. What do you do in this situation? Affirm and make sure you let them know you are still in the equation and you are not going anywhere.

Worried

How will you make ends meet? You are the only one working. The things you have to do too keep the insurance adjuster from cutting off the checks. Every month a threat if they don't get the medical documents from the doctor's office they will cut him off. This was every other week; how do you make a doctor's receptionist do what she is supposed to do? Change doctors; find one that is responsible.

Tears

Could it be that a stroke is what God used to configure your mind? I remember after Donnie's stroke, he would cry a lot after a reply. I want to see my family; he knew they were far but just wanted to see them. So the need and want was still there for him. He would cry, his mind couldn't wrap around hundreds of miles away. A call would have sufficed, he really missed his older brother who would call to see how his baby bro was doing. That would put a smile on his face and tears in his eyes. The tears soften his heart to hear God's voice; he had become more spiritual than I have seen him be in all the years I have been with him. He had become so compassionate and very thankful of what was done for him. God uses everything I truly believe that.

No Help (I Need Help)

You hope for help, no help in or out of the family—consistent help not sometime help. Not help when it is convenient for you. What can be done hook up with groups that have similar problems you have to share for support. There is some time outside groups that can give you a time to get out and relieve you from some stress of the day. When I got home from work, I told my husband I am going to my bedroom to get some down time, and when I felt like it, I would check in with him. He still could feed himself, but I had to help with toiletry.

Don't Run Away

Many times when a person doesn't understand a situation, the easy or automatic thing to do is run. Let's run from the issue you are running away from a person that is in need. The next time you are confronted with sickness in your family, please don't run from that person. Picking up a phone and checking on how they are doing will put a smile on their face and let them know they are still in your thoughts, that they are not forgotten Running away and no communication is the most hurtful thing that can happen to a disabled person.

Out of Sight, Out of Mind

A slogan that many people are adhering to these days. If I don't see a problem, then there is no problem. What a lie from the devil, the help the person needs that is help for caregivers. This is the pass for the person to not engage in the person's life.

Question

Why when you confront a lady about her relationship with God, she automatically, if they are in a relationship, turns the focus to their spouse's walk with God or lack of it. We have to know and believe we are not our husband's savior. Everybody is responsible for their own soul's salvation.

Wife, Caregiver, and Widow

I was a kept wife, meaning my husband Donnie took care of everything. I didn't have to want for food, clothing, all our needs were met. If we didn't have it, then and there, he worked to get the things we needed for his family. He paid bills, I didn't have to do that, he worked, I didn't have to do that, we came together as one, not easy, but it was durable, and not happy all the time, but he was my best friend, and we had a love that grew from teenage to adulthood. That's the reason that when he became disabled, it was not a question in my mind to not care for him in any and all the way I could. Was it easy? No, some days were harder than others, but I settled in my mind it was three against the world. My granddaughter which I know without her and the Lord, I would have flown the coop. All the prayers from my mother which is a surviving widow that knew all the feelings I was going through. She tried to shelter me like she always tried, but this was a road nobody but me could travel and fill all the bumps and bruises. While my husband couldn't really get around much or he couldn't fix his food, I would do all of that before I would leave for work and pray all the time I was away that he wouldn't fall or die while I was away from home. I made sure the shades was open, so he could see the sun and made sure his Animal Planet was on the TV also. He didn't know how to turn the channels or his hands wouldn't work right, so he couldn't operate. I got used to him not calling me at work, saying, "What you doing?"

He went on dialysis, and we both agreed that we would do this at home after seeing how his close friend suffered at the facility from dialysis, and tubes kept coming out of her. We wouldn't have to worry about how he would get back and forth to the facility. Physically, it was just us almost a year on dialysis. I had got the hang of it if it wasn't for FMLA on my job, I would have lost it. Because sometimes, the machine had me up throughout the night calling Baxter for help. I would be too sleepy to get up so I had that advantage. This didn't happen all the time, just a couple times. My daughter, Donnetta, took the dialysis training with me that really helped as a backup. I am so glad that on April 3, 2016, we went to Donnie's favorite restaurant; my son had given him a gift card for Christmas. Afterward is when he passed from the earthly home to his heavenly home. Absent from the body is present with the Lord. This has helped me from the time of Donnie's death to now. 2 Corinthians 5:6–8 God love the widows. Psalms 68:5. I will take some time for my heart to heal; we was together for thirty-nine yrs. Many people said we wouldn't make it because we were eighteen and nineteen years old, too young back then. I wouldn't advise any young couple to marry at a young age because it's hard to get a place to rent and credit. You have to have people sign for you. I see now that I am at the fork of the road by myself without my best friend, I will do okay but it will take time. I don't know how long, but it is hard especially when you have no support and it is an uphill climb. I would rather be in labor twenty-four hours than be without Donnie. Even though at the end, he wasn't able to do like he wanted for himself. He still was a great man with his mind still intact. Another thing I must say, before you get married, know as much about your soon-to-be in-laws, build a relationship throughout before and after marriage, so when this time comes, you know that your in-laws got your back and you can call if they can't come to see about you there is support there because that is needed after a spouse dies. There is a slogan in the world that says, "I am not marrying your family, I am marrying you." That is a lie from the pit; everybody becomes part of your marriage, and denying it don't make it go away. It would have made a world of difference; my brother-in laws and their wives would not have dropped the ball on us. Live and learn.

Loneliness

This is the worse feeling I think you can have. It cut to the core of your heart. Loneliness comes in stages; when you least expect it, the feeling engulfs you. What do you do to fill the void? Walk until the feeling subsides, exercise, stay away from food if you can don't need the extra pounds. Meet new people and learn to socialize. This is a lost art, socializing in public and not social media. Question: will I ever find something to feel this void? I refuse to be ignored. I will fight to keep my head up and not wait on others to take me out, take your own self out. One young lady said she was traveling out of town by herself because if she waited for someone to take her anywhere, she wouldn't go. Smart young lady, just because you had a houseful of kids, don't expect them to dote on you or be there at your beck and call; what universe do you live on. Make yourself happy; don't wait for others to do it.

Widowhood

God should be our focus since being a widow I have read all types of widow's responses after their husband dies.

- He was my whole life.
- I can't live or breathe without him.
- I can't think of living without him.
- I can't live me without him.

I would tell a young couple that is racing to the altar, "Please, please don't put them on a pedestal. That is a spot only for God. You should know that God is the reason you are breathing, don't hold your spouse so tight. Hold them loosely."

Thirty-Nine Years

I would never have thought that people that you have known thirty-nine years would just forget you, no call to see if you are living or dead. I know men don't usually think of things like that, but women are usually more feeling and compassionate I would think not! I am only responsible for my thoughts. This mind-set will stop your flow of healing. Opening up how you feel while going through grief helps also. I was raised in a generation where the belief was if you don't say nothing, it will go away. Now I believe in freeing myself less stress. Just listen and be there to share Kleenex; a response is not always needed.

Showing me your puppy dog eyes and sad face look and patting me on my back was the most aggravating thing I experienced.

This widowhood is a road I hate to be on; no one picks this club, but if you can find people with like situations, this road will be less rocky. Develop a strong support group; can't rush the grief process. My personality is that I want it over real quick because I don't like to hurt.

It's Not the Same

You will notice that the friends that you and your husband had together after he has passed on the friendship may change. If the person is not secure in their relationship, jealousy arises and you can't be with them anymore. You have to make new friends. That's if you have insecure friends and the thing about this you won't know until after the passing of your spouse. Just a heads up, don't ask your friends' husband for any help, no tire changes, get a roadside membership. Don't ask them to shovel your snow, check our water faucet in the house, no way. It's better to pay someone for help around the house than to cause problems. As innocent as it may sound, that can be a problem. I have talked to other women that have lost their husbands, and they have told me that they were friends with couples for years, but when her husband passed, the wife dropped her friendship with her and would not allow her husband to check her car for any problems, which he used to do. I call that a hen-pecked man and a insecure woman. I don't know what makes women think that all of a sudden, after our spouse passes, we are now going to be the whore of Babylon and try to take all the married men; what a stupid assumption. Keep it moving, there other friends for you to make. Don't fret over this, this is very common.

Melt Down

I am one to try to get things over quickly grief is not one of the things to try to push it through fast. I experienced this on a weekend I had to leave my home, and everything was making me cry. I have heard the grief counselors say this over and over, but I wasn't listening. I know me. I thought if I could get through this tiresome grief then I could get on with my new life (wrong). Take the grief road slow; don't rush. It just might come back and bite you.

The Contract Is Over

When you have a clause in your vows until death do us part. Easier said than done especially when you weren't looking for an exit door. I know for sure that when it's over and death separates us from our spouse. The heart has to heal from that departure; there is nothing on this earth that can touch or heal this open wound that you have. The only thing that will soothe the hurt is time with God. But I know a human being can't close that hole. You can't rush it; remember, take your time to heal.

Didn't Ask to Be a Widow

Even though I was my husband's caregiver for four years, I didn't ask to be a widow. I loved getting home and he would be waiting for me on the couch. I expected to fix his dinner when I got home. Toward the end, his appetite was not much so I didn't have to cook a lot. I won't lie, I was tired some days more than others, but I never wished to be a widow; who does that? Since I've been a widow and noticed that this is one group, the widows/widowers that don't get much support from others; don't expect them to. They don't know how this journey feels so don't expect them to feel the void or hurt not going to happen. So thankful the widows' community is so huge, we can draw support and strength from our sisters and brothers that know how deep our pain is. Most people will say get over it after hanging around for two weeks or a month.

Don't Lose Yourself

Please, please, I can't stress this more, women, don't lose yourself in your husband. I understand man being the head, I understand two flesh becoming one. I also understand when your spouse's head is cold and you can't see him or hear his voice. I hope you have your identity in check, that what God gave didn't die when your husband died. Keep your friends when you married, balance your time with them and time with your family. This will help in the long run if you live by the old adage "my four and no more, "you might be left behind holding nothing because of no relationship building outside the household. Sometimes, friendships outlive our spouses; please don't make your spouse your idol.

There Is Still a Widow in the House

I don't know why people stop coming over to visit when the spouse dies. I can remember my sweet mother-in-law had a man visit her every Sunday evening or other days. I asked my husband why did this man come and visit his mother every weekend or other days, sometimes just sitting and not saying anything. He said well, he was friends with his father, and after his father died, he always came by the house to check on the family to make sure they were okay. Well, nowadays, you can't get blood relatives to come to the house to check or call you; those days are gone in the wind, so sad. Does it hurt to come in the house? Imagine how the widow feels living day after day looking at the spot where he no longer sits. Before you think of how hard it is for you to go to the house, think about the widow that still lives there. That is why I had to move. I couldn't live in the place me and Donnie shared; it was too hard. The advise they give widows not to make hasty decisions after spouse passes, but that was the one I had to make was to move. I was in a daze, but with the help of God and moving service, we were able to do it.

Widowness/Singleness

The loneliness of eating alone you will never know if you have not been there. The first time I would want to sit in a secluded area away from hustle and bustle. This could be good, but too far, you could be forgotten by the waitress. I used to wonder about ten years ago and I would see a person eating by themselves and say to myself how could they do it, I could never do that. Don't never say never. Say I hope I don't have to go down that road of doing things by myself. I hope that doesn't happen to me, I also noticed that people (waitresses) are extremely nice to you when you sit by yourself.

It's Their Problem, Not Yours

Don't wonder if your married friends are dodging you or not inviting you to different functions, the relationship is not the same since your spouse has passed. Please don't think it's your fault; it is their insecurity that makes them not trust their mate around you. I know my boundaries; you will never see me with a married man outside work unless he is with his wife, don't set yourself up. As innocent as it is, unless it is okay with the wife for you to be talking with her husband, don't do it.

Please Be Advised

Things change, it doesn't stay the same. The new normal. I hate change, it configures my plans that I have set in my mind. Friendships change. I have learned to make new friends and don't share your widow experience with people that are not widows/widowers. I only share with my pastor and my family. Keep in mind everybody is not for you and can't relate to your issue.

Were you ever introduced as "That's David's wife, Michael's wife, Keith's wife"? Well, now that's the time that you should say "No, I am Rita or Barbara or your name." Say your name, say your name. I think we have used the marriage as an excuse to lose ourselves, and when and if the loss of the other person, it is hard for you to see yourself as an individual; don't lose yourself. If you are doing all you are supposed to do, this is not for you; this is only for the ones that have lost themselves in their spouse and now can't branch off to what your purpose is. Get unstuck now and rise to what you are supposed to do in this new normal.

The Eraser

He came when I was hurt by two of the most powerful men in my life. My father and my uncle. The word jealousy and deception and promises broken. When I graduated from high school, I was promised a car to get back and forth from college. It was snatched from me because of what my uncle told my father. My uncle said, "Your daughter is very disrespectful, that's what they do when they get a little education." The spirit of jealousy reared its ugly head that not only destroyed me but my family. We were never the same after that. His daughter didn't go to college, so this is how this started. But he was my favorite; surely he is not doing this. I saw and heard all of this. We were visiting my grandparents; my father had gotten a beautiful car for my graduation and while there long story short. My father took the car back with the help of my uncle driving it back to Michigan with his wife because my father thought I was being disrespectful. He was the younger brother that looked up to his brother and believed what he said. The car was a burgundy Monte Carlo 1976 white interior.

Well, when I married Donnie, he tried to erase the hurt that I still was feeling; he went and bought a blue Monte Carlo white interior. He knew how I loved that car; we were just starting out young and had just moved in an apartment in Florida; well, it was hard to keep everything afloat with two small babies. I think we had that car a little over a year we had to let it go. That didn't hurt like the first time, and amazingly, I never had another want or feeling for another car like that. The more I thought he would always try to fill the area where I hurt. He was my eraser of the bad. Now I am not saying that we had a perfect all good relationship, but I am saying that the good outweighed the bad. Just as soon as Donnie came in my life was as fast as he left. God knew what I needed at the time. I wouldn't have been able to raise my kids with all the hurt and back stabbing that I had endured from family. Thank God that he used Donnie to help with the healing process. You don't know how you have come along until you stop and look at the process. Set your pace for healing; it is coming in ways you least expect.

The First

All the previous firsts that I went through got me ready for the final first. The first Fourth, he used to do the BBQ for us, but he stopped soon before the stroke; he said the smell was getting to him. The blow of him not being here is not as bad as if he was suddenly gone. I had to step in and do when he was no longer able to do. The stroke leveled the ground and lessened the blow of him not being here with me anymore. I am walking through the first birthday without him and him calling everyone to remind them to wish your mom a happy birthday, and each of my kids would call and wish me a happy birthday. He would also have my daughter go and get him a card for me and maybe flowers or candy that is missing. Now the next biggy, the first anniversary.

Reaping the Benefit

That is a phrase you think of as a long-time off thing. If your spouse leaves you some kind of benefit. The benefit is to sustain you while you still have to do life. He thought enough of you to look beyond their present time and set papers to cover things for you when he would be no longer with you. What a final act of love, you have to cherish from your spouse.

No Feelings

Let me educate you before you get your feelings hurt. Don't ask a widow/widower what are you planning on doing on your BD/

Anniversary especially when it's the first. You might get a crazy answer back or you might get looked at like you are short, you might get a response that will hurt. Unreal. SMH.

Yep, You Are on the Lonely Road

You try to get people involve with this widow road with you, but that is not going to happen they only go so far if they go at all. But in reality, you were the only one that entered in matrimony with your spouse. You the only one that knew when he stopped feeling like he couldn't make it another day. You saw him falling on the bathroom floor. All the feelings that you shared you knew, so how can others share this walk? You have to set this one out alone, carve the road, and allow the Holy Spirit to guide to soothe and to comfort.

The Farewell Letter

This is the last exercise that was done at one of my grief classes. We wrote a letter to our spouse and later burning the letter.

> Dear Donnie,
> When we met at Atlanta College, I never knew that you were the one until you kept following me and my friends. I was trying to get away, but you kept on until you caught my heart. I remember telling my teacher in high school that I was moving to Atlanta to go to school there and marry a Georgia man and have children. That is the way it went for us. Boom. Boom. Boom. I admired how you stepped up to the plate. When I told you I was pregnant, you didn't miss a beat, you said, "Let's do this," meaning, "Let's get married." You were a great father and husband at nineteen years old. You never ran away from your responsibilities. I remember the first car you had when you came

to visit me over the weekend from Florida. I would hear the blue Volkswagen coming up the road. You had every chance to abandon your responsibility, but you didn't miss a beat. You graduated and went to Florida to get a job coming back and forth to Atlanta. Thank you for the dedication that you had for our family. I thank you for raising boys to be strong men and caring fathers and a daughter with a heart big as yours. We had a lot of arguments when our kids were young about how they should be raised, but we figured it out. We got married so young that people said we wouldn't make it, but we made a lie out of them all. I want to thank you for my four babies, thank you for all the hours you worked to make our life better. Sometimes working three different jobs to make ends meet. There were times when we moved up to Detroit and you would have to walk down dark streets in Detroit to catch two buses because you sold your car to get a bus ticket to move with us to Detroit. The cold winters your first experience dealing with this type of weather didn't stop you. You borrowed one of your coworker's car sometime to get groceries and toys for the kids around Christmas time. You did all this to keep a roof over our head and food on the table without any handouts. Thank you for allowing me to stay home with my children to make sure they were okay and getting back and forth to school, all the baseball games, basketball games, and practices. Paying for kids to go to private school so they could have safe and quality education. You never looked for anything back, you were raised to take care of your family and that is what you did. You were my strong shoulder guy, I could come to you when I was distraught over anything; you would listen and give advice. My Big D, a big heart with much compassion. Now I know why we had our family so fast, we would tell people the reason we had our children so fast is because we wanted to grow up with them and then laughed about it. This is why when you had a stroke, I never batted an eye; it was no question, you would never be put in convalescent home. Hey, you showed me how to cook and cut up a chicken. The least I could do was take care of your needs and wants. With the help of God, it was us three against the world. If I had the chance, I would do it all over again. I don't regret nothing, Donnie. It's like God allowed you to stay with me those years after the stroke to make sure I would be okay with taking care of the bills and all of the other things that needed to be done. I know that you were tired of sitting in one spot on the sofa while everyone was going on their way with their life and you were there just watching TV day in and day out. I know and you know this was not the Donnie I married, I am glad you accepted the Lord as your Savior after all the years of witnessing with and without words. I cherish the mornings when we prayed, and you would always pray and say, "Lord, let my wife get to work safe and don't let nobody bother her." We would kiss and say goodbye. I would sit at work many days praying that you wouldn't fall when or if you did get up. Well, I know now that when I was praying for total healing, you were asking God to let you come home. Baby, I am okay. I will see you again when this life is over. I still miss you, but I won't be mad at you no more. You are no longer suffering or in pain, you are present with our Lord and Savior Jesus Christ.

Love,
Your wife
Ruby

This letter helped to release a lot and got me unstuck, then we burned the letter as a symbol.

Donnie enjoying the outside with Leilani.

Donnie loved walking by the water.

He seldom took pictures without putting up his
hand to hide. He was glad to take this one.

Donnie took this picture shortly after he bought this bike. He
had gotten interested in riding shortly before the stroke.

Grief

A word you don't want to deal with. This affects everyone in the family. But the loss of a spouse, your soul mate that you have bonded with for so many years. This tears at the soul. I am having to get past the looking back at the things that was not done for him, so I know what wasn't done for him; it will trigger down to me. I won't get the support for him from death. Grieving by yourself is the grief that I hate because it seems to me to be so long.

Stuck

One word that is used after your spouse has crossed over. I was with him so long, I knew when he was turning in the driveway. I heard him get home before he physically got there. I used to hear my grandmother say that about my granddad. I thought she was crazy, but it was so true. I had plans. Now what do I do? I am stuck for that adventure, pull me through, so how can I carry on. It is something that just because you are stuck, you are still moving forward. The first year is a daze, the second you feel everything. Just doing to be doing. I can do this with or without help from outside forces. Help me, help me, pull me through, Lord.

Learning to Live Again

I can't change the circumstances of life; many people are mad at their love one for leaving them behind. Left to cope the misery of being alone. How to recreate yourself, how to start over again. Couples, please don't come this way, go the other way. I am hurting, of all the times, of all the places. Why this way, why next to me. A living torture, will this be over? This is what I would think in my mind about two years of being a widow. I am much better now four years out.

Cooking Singular

That's a chore in itself. I have fed the garbage more than I have fed myself, the garbage eats good. I had to learn to singularly freeze things so the food wouldn't go bad. The appetite goes up and down. The change and variations of food change too. I might have an idea of what I want for dinner, but let a coworker or TV ad come on, my taste bud changes to what I have just heard. Weird.

Can Anybody See What I Am Going Through

And neither do they care because they are going through a different path also. Many people say after the funeral, no phone calls, no visits, what about during the caregiving time, there is no call from relatives or friends. There is no call to see if you are okay or need anything. I really don't know how strong God wants me because from lifting an over two hundred pounds man from chair to seat and now moving a small container with his ashes, I don't get no help at all. My help comes from the Lord who made heaven and earth. People (family see) and don't see. Out of sight, out of mind.

Seeing in the Eyes of Just You

So many times when married, you focus on us and now the focus is on me (singular); it is sometimes hard to think singular. To regroup and see the world in a singular mind is so hard after thirty-nine years being in a group dynamics; how do you cook singular, think singular, live singular, talk singular. Just do it until the new normal aligns itself to you.

Loneliness

Why is it that when your spouse dies, people put you away as being dead also? I don't understand this at all. If you don't call or go by their house, they sure won't check on you. This is the new normalcy because this is not just happening to me but to quite a few other widows I have heard from.

Believe what People Do

Listen to what people say, don't try to push yourself on people. If people give you a short response to your questions, that is a sign they don't want to be bothered and your presence is no longer needed, goodbye. When people consistently lie to you, that's a sign that they don't want to be in your life. Excuse them, that means blood or not blood. The blood people will hurt you more than the non-blood people because it cuts to the core. You don't expect it, but it is happening a lot now from talking to others; this is the real world

We Are the Strong Ones

I ask myself why there are so many women that are left behind. Why are there more women caregivers for husbands than the other way around? I thought we were the weaker sex but seems like we are strong when going through the trials of everyday life; we are strong when we go through sickness. When raising children, we are strong; even when we are sick ourselves, we continue to go. We usually have to take care of ourselves even if someone is in the house, not to mention if all have passed. I think I will get a home device that will call emergency if I have fallen and can't get up.

Those Holidays

If I could take the holidays, the birthdays, and celebrations out of the years, I think I could make it without the lows and mood swings. If I could just go down this path without facing Donnie's birthday, our anniversary, and Fourth of July; he used to love to BBQ before he had the stroke. If I could skip Christmas at the end he loved, but before the stroke, he didn't. I will just sit by the water from sun up to sundown. I will just stay in my room and nap until the next day. You will get through the first year was the worse, but as the time goes by, it comes and goes; everybody is different, your experience might last longer.

You Grasp for a Life Jacket

I find that when you try to share your life struggles with someone you think is listening, you get a drop the mike moment. Case being:

> Sister: How have you been, Ruby?
> Me: Well, I really have been hurting.

No response really, the text was never responded to really.

I don't think there is one person that can walk this road with you, no matter how much you have put in a relationship when it's your time, you are left abandoned. No matter who you want to drag down the road of grief you are going through by yourself and the almighty God if you choose. If I didn't have him holding me up, this would and could be a time of giving up.

A Different Perspective on Death

I am speaking on the side of the left-behind spouse. I am viewing only from this perspective have you ever thought of just maybe my spouse left because of the expiration for their life came to a halt. Maybe the life they were living on this side was not productive for them or you. Maybe you were taking a different road. After my husband died, I saw a fork in the road, a path we once walked together now is a fork where we are traveling without each other. My goodness, what am I supposed to do now? It's all about me, I am the healthier one, so I put myself in my husband's shoes. I was leaving out the house every day to work it like we traded places; now he was at home sitting on the sofa all day looking at TV. He was scared to get up, scared he would fall. He kept a urinal beside him and held his bowel when he could. This was a very clean man in his healthier days. Out of all the thirty-nine years of marriage, I only smelled his

BO when I became his caregiver. Now he was so prideful of his cleanliness. So with all this going on in his mind, he can't drive anymore, he couldn't walk where he wanted. He was always thinking of falling, he was dizzy all the time. He couldn't fix his own food. I am putting myself in his shoes. Could he have made his peace with God and asked to be taken home. I am just saying it's very possible when we want our loved one not to leave us; we are thinking about our selfish selves couldn't that be possible, of other things also, but change the perspective; look at it through their eyes.

It's a New Path

A path I know I wouldn't travel alone. There is a fork in the road, which way do I go: the right or left. I can't find you to hold your hand. I can't ask you if this is the right way, but I know I have to physically travel this road alone without you at my side.

Loneliness

It's a shame that loneliness can be your friend to think and to wonder. Why is it that many parents have children that are so disrespectful at their old age? Holler curses at them and their children do the same. Wonder where they would have made it without their parents' help. Now that's a wonder many have gotten doctorates, and do you think they invite them out for dinner, no, God forbid now, the parents are in the way.

The Curve, The Turn

What is your turn/curve? It's that time to laugh and move on. Move on while in your mind there is and was a time of other times. Please find something you can laugh at or find humor in. Laughter is medicine to your soul. I am a type of person I look and question almost everything in my mind. I might not say anything about it. I let it roll around in my mind. Then I think about different scenarios.

What would happen if I did this instead of that, now that will drive you crazy second-guessing yourself.

Also get into something that make your blood boil and you have so much compassion for that if you don't get involved in it, it won't get done. Find something to do that will demand you to work on it until it is complete. Work until the end, don't give up the fight. You know it is complete it is not benefiting the community that is not noticing, but you are completing a work that is benefiting a well-needed community.

What is the motivation of your drive? Is it to please you and lift you up or is it to benefit those around you and helping others to reach their goals and dreams, be the motor that drive you and others.

Laugh a lot, don't stress over the small incidents in life, help someone to reach their dream.

I have settled it in my mind to get over the fact that my in-laws, my husband's brothers, have written us off and one of my support team have said that 90 percent of widows are deserted by in-laws is not a new thing. One lady said that right after the funeral, there was no contact. Another widow said that she was sorry they left and ignored her, but she had other people in her life that it didn't bother her; at first, it did, but later, she adjusted to it. Another widow said that if you didn't release and forgive, your soul would hurt forever for this kind of pain. So as of this day, I will not linger over the desertion. I will move on and try to forget that part of my life. In the words of one of my kids, they said, "Mama, his brothers never kept in contact with Dad when we were kids, so why are you stressing about it now?" So why would they contact his family and kids now. So true, never thought of that.

Don't Let Grief Make a Fool Out of You

When an over-occurrence of sadness comes and you don't expect it.

When you are so sad that you can't move or proceed to everyday life.

When you are so miserable, you can't see hope in your life or in anyone else's life.

Learning to accept your never overcoming or unstoppable sadness.

Let's put Bible scripture to these to bust this up and you can quote these scriptures to get you through getting one. Words can help in these situations.

It's time to think on something that make you think.

Laughter is surely medicine. This is a section that I have witnessed personally or others have experienced.

Why do people expect you to have a pasted smile on your face 24/7? I had a friend that wore this pasted smile on her face from morning to night, and she expected me to have that same smile on my face too. I had to tell her one day, "Why would I have a smile on my face 24/7 when you are smiling enough for both of us?" Now don't get me wrong, my characteristic is not to have a pasted smile on my face all the time. I know that the joy of the Lord is our strength. But please don't get it twisted, just because you don't see the smile doesn't mean I am absent of joy.

Isn't it funny how some people see life differently? Some people say I am going through an adventure when they are broke and busted; now I say this is no adventure nothing adventurous about seeing how to stretch your dollars and fighting with the bill collectors; miss me with that word please.

Why I didn't listen you said they weren't worth two dead flies without wings. So true when a mother put the wants and desires of a man that is what equates to a useless mother.

I should have listened when you said don't worry about her, it's just us against the world, let's just think of us.

I should have listened when you said oh, I was given away, I was left and was just said goodbye to without even checking on me.

I should have listened when you said she is not going to do any better. she has done this for years.

What do I do put all my beliefs on this one person and is slapped in the face with I told you so.

Didn't you know the grass is greener on the other side? Why is that because their family is so good, always there, never missing.

Didn't you know the sky is bluer because their husband is living, always giving them flowers, always taking them out on dates?

Didn't you know that the cool air blows on them better than me because they have a great home?

Now to know that the husband is trying to do everything to make up for cheating on her for many years, the sky is cloudier now.

Now to know that the house was in default and threatening a bankruptcy; there is no cool air but humidity is in the horizon.

Stop looking at others when the outward perspectives are sometime faulty; a lot of people are just barely making it.

When is it going to stop? Your child is thirty years old is still draining your account, she's leaving you with no money.

When is it going to stop driving your thirty years old to work; your car brakes have just went out.

When is it going to stop, you are laying in the hospital bed for the fifth time and no visit, no recognition of you.

When is it going to stop, it just did. Here lies the unthoughtful, unappreciated, forgetful mother RIP Mother.

Thank you for the pushback, thank you for the neglect, thank you for ignoring me, thank you for not calling, thank you for not visiting, thank you for all the lies that we are going here there and everywhere, thank you because in all of the hurt this pushed me to get this done; in all of this, it has made me give birth to my new life. What is a negative in your life will push you to a new positive, a new you that had to be done.

Relationships

Ask yourself why am I in a relationship? Is it to help me to get me further in my life or is it to help me or help him? How much will you take before you call it quits? It depends on you. I used to tell people, a man will go as far as you let him go. Women, you write the ticket. Men, after looking, will take a lot just to keep a women from taking what is so dear to him. But that will only last but awhile. Don't give your peace up to pacify someone else; life is too short.

There Is More than One

I wonder why the focus is just on one when you have several kids, you don't think that just maybe the others need help.

The others need a helping hand; before you make that mistake in focusing on one, distribute your focus on the others. When they show you that your help is not respected anymore, that's your time to switch up and focus on your others that is in your life.

The Season Is Over

It is not intended for you to carry the same people you started with to end with sometime. Friendship is sometimes long term, short term; you have to know when to stay or run. In my time of aloneness, I have seen a lot of hurting people that hurt people, and since I have gotten to this age now, I don't waste my time staying in a relationship with someone that doesn't want to be bothered.

Brighter Days Are Coming

That's one of the sayings that my pastor used to say all the time and so it is the cloud has lifted and there is light at the end of the tunnel. There was no A, B, C step in doing things, no formula. You have to move the way is good for you to get through; everyone is different. But do know you are coming out.

Finally I got the response, this is why.

This is why I haven't heard from my brother-in-laws; you can't get blood from a turnip. Donnie was the baby boy in the family, but he was also the one that helped his mother farm the land. I remember him telling me before he passed that one of his brothers was sickly and the other ran the street, leaving the duty to help his mother around the house. So that in itself tells you they were not there to put in his life or had relationship with him. So how in the world can they today be there for his family if not but for communication? They can't because they weren't there for Donnie so that explains why they can't be there for his sons. It's a generation thing and I pray that I have broken that off my sons that they will not do that to the next generation. I see my adult kids put others before themselves. I can honestly say they give and look out for others without a problem. It's not to be expected anymore because you can't get blood from a turnip. This has taught me not to expect people to give you anything, just an ear to listen, no monetary thing. I don't care how long you have known them. It's a difference from knowing of a person but not having a relationship in the years that you have known that person. I had a dream of Donnie walking with me, and I told him, "Donnie, you know your brothers have not called to see if we were okay and just to say hello to me or your our kids."

He just said, "Well, you know our family are not that kind to check up on each other," and that was all he said, he was not surprised. Now I don't dream about Donnie at all. I believe that the Holy Spirit was answering my long question that I was always wondering since Donnie died. The why no response, have I done something, did I forget someone's name on the obituary, what was it. And when I woke up that morning, this is what I heard in my spirit: you can't get blood from a turnip; don't expect what people can't give. Don't be wondering about this anymore; move on and let it go. I felt the peace of now knowing the why and I can move on.

The Time Frame

Why it is taking me so long to complete this book is because I am facing things and opening up wounds that I just don't want to be open again. Going back to a childhood to see that one of my uncle's remarks changed the whole equation of our family. "You don't know what your daughter will be" saying this to my father. Jealousy is as cruel as the grave.

This Now Generation

I was talking to one of my sister girls the other day, and she was telling me that she hadn't heard from her kids in a while; they stay out of town. I had the same situation with mine; we don't converse every day, but we do talk. I had my youngest make a message for all of us to be able to connect so we could jump on to see if all is well after the Covid epidemic broke out, an easy way to connect and to see if all is well and we are still alive. But getting back, this generation don't check on their elderly like the baby boomers and before; as always there are some exception to the rule. You adjust and that is sad because when it's over, it's over.

The Widow's Brain Is So Real

I have checked myself over and over again, making sure I turned the stove off or making sure I closed the garage door. One day, I left the door opened overnight, now no one in my community came over to tell me the garage was opened. Everybody over here is to themselves. I never see anyone coming over to talk with their neighbors, that is weird to me; they wave a lot but don't neighbor visit, maybe it's the way of the world now.

When I was going through the time of being a caregiver and then widow, my concentration was very bad, but I know I needed a life support to lead and guide me, but it was hard for me to read a whole scripture; the concentration was bad, I couldn't focus so it was impressed on me that God's word breaks all yokes and bondages. He didn't say the amount of the words but his word. So I grasped on one word from God and it helped me keep my head above water; hope this will help you.

Thirty One Words

When going through this path, caregiver to widow, your attention span can be so short, you can't focus. The following words may describe what you felt or are feeling and that one verse can help turn that situation around in your mind. This is the issue: can't focus to read, to do anything that you need to, but I could have one word that I could hold on to, to get through that is attached to the word of God; it helped me survive. I didn't write the whole scripture out because I used to hate to buy a book finding out when I get it home, it is full of scripture; it was like I was buying another Bible. This way you can get your own Bible translation or app and follow the scriptures that way. Add your sentence to what you need to do in this word and add your scripture base and issue.

Hope

In all things, there is a glimpse of hope it will get better.
Mark 5:35–36; Psalms 31:24

Help

When all else is looking like nothing is there for me.
Psalm 30:2; 33:20

Rest

You have to regain your strength.
Psalm 127:2

Tired

From running back and forth.
Galatians 6:9; 2 Thessalonians 3:13

Understand

You are making life a little bit better for the one that can't do better for themselves.
Job 36:29; Proverb 30:18–19

Regroup

Bringing things together that make sense for that day.
Psalms 46:10; 2 Chronicles 20:17

Silence

When there is nothing more to say.
Psalm 46:10–11

Prepare

Do all the things you know to do and the things you were told to do to get through life.
Genesis 41:28–36

Problems

This is a teaching/learning moment.
James 1:2–4

Thoughts

What is on your mind?
Philippians 4:8

Laughter

Proverbs 17:12

Faith

This is running thin, can't see what we need to see;
tiredness is trying to pull this down.
Romans 5:1–11

Time

This waits for no one;
say what you need to and do what you got to do.
Ecclesiastes 3:1; 7:14; 8:5

Promises

God fulfills all his promises, and they bring peace.
Mark 1:2–3

Always

The Lord will never leave us.
Matthew 28:20

Anxiety

Feeling rushed, everything is coming at me, can't figure it out.
Psalm 139:23; Philippians 4:6; 1 Peter 5:7

Believe

Is there going to be enough money to take care all the needs?
Roman 4:20

Sleepless nights

From things running around your mind.
Psalms 3:5; Philippians 4:19; Luke 10:41–42;
2 Corinthians 4:8–9; Romans 8:28

Unfairness

Why me; why do we have to be going through this?
Life isn't always fair.
Ecclesiastes 9:10–11

Worry

Don't worry about it; pray always about it.
Philippians 4:6–7

Finished

Done over doesn't mean a negative thing. Jesus said this word, and that's when a new, good thing started for all.
John 19:30

Guilt

After everything is over, this one comes in your mind.
Philippians 3:13–14

Hopelessness

May feel like this when there is no support.
Psalms 69:13

Prayer

Conversation with God.
Mark 11:24; 1 John 5:14–15; Isaiah 65:24; Psalm 55:17

Strength

Needing this desperately
Psalms 23:3; 28:7; 84:5; Habakkuk 3:19;
Philippians 4:13; Hebrews 11:33–34

Alone

No one to share my hurting.
John 14:18; Isaiah 58:9; 2 Corinthians 6:18

Guilt

Thoughts of did I do enough?
If I did, they would have gotten better.
1 John 3:20

Peace

Need this in an upside-down situation.
Colossians 3:15; Psalms 85:8; Philippians 4:7; John 14:27

Directionless

Don't know which way to turn; never done this before.
Proverbs 3:5–6; 1 Peter 5:7; Psalm 84:11–12

Wait

Don't rush; be patient.
Psalm 40:1; Exodus 2:23–25

Acknowledgments

God is surely still molding me on this path. I give him praise and thanksgiving for what he has done in me and through me.

I want to thank my mother, Lucille Denson, for all the prayers and consolation she gave me doing this time. A powerful prayer warrior. My brother, Samuel Denson, for being so patient with Donnie for consolation.

Thanks for my grown kids, that followed the guidance and didn't fall far from the tree, Maurice, Donnetta, DJ, Jonathan Daggett and Nita his daughter in love always glad to see and Ash who he loved to joke with. My little stone that kept me together before and after Leilani Daggett; all my grandsons, Howard B. Brandon and Lil Maurice that use to keep Papa up with your online games. Our granddaughters, Hailey, Haleia, Lily, Mya and Leilani that pampered him doing his nails and hair when he was in rehab

Ernest and Janice Davis, long-time friends from birth of our boys to now have always been there. Giving and never expecting anything in return

Thanks to my sister girls, Laura Bowlson, who had all night prayers and Bible studies that kept me going. My two sisters, Rose Brewer and Tina Boyd, who gave me encouragement and support and helped me to stay grounded. Marsha Moseley and Faye Deh, the three musketeers who keep me laughing and traveling.

Thanks to Denise, The First Lady, her husband passed a week before mine; we were holding up each other at the grief group.

Pastor Yolanda Tyson and the Cathedral of Love Church Family for being there for me and covering me in prayers and support. She also would come to my home to give Donnie communion.

All my Eastwood neighbors and friends that was there for Donnie when I was at work. Tommy and Patricia Starks, real solid friends, Pat supplied food for Donnie, and Tommy picked Donnie up when he fell; LaNaysha and her boys, Amir and Uriah, that would take time with him keeping him company; James for being his road runner partner; Chinetha and her mom; and Cindy and Jim keeping him company.

About the Author

Ruby Daggett is a mother of four adults and has ten grandchildren and two great-grandchildren. Ruby married at nineteen years old to Donnie Daggett. In her free time, she loves to be near the river and just meditate. Her getaway on road trips is one of the things she loves to do on the weekends. Getting together with friends to share a time to get together is also what she enjoys. Ruby likes to wind down from a busy day with a good movie. Doing her earlier years, she had bible studies in her home with ladies, also being involved with different prayer groups.

She was raised by a strong woman who showed her how, not to worry, but to pray. This has now been her motto in life—"before you start to worry, pray about it because prayer is the answer to all problems". She enjoys crocheting and cooking.

Ruby went to various colleges when she was younger. She was trying to see where her interests were as she went to take the test to get into nursing school but missed the entrance by one point. She set her mind to further her education, but with the children needing her the most, she put that on the back burner. She did what was most important, to be there one hundred percent for her family.

CPSIA information can be obtained
at www.ICGtesting.com
Printed in the USA
BVHW050618230321
603242BV00017B/1583

9 781098 078430